D1623139

THE BABY BONDING BOOK FOR DADS

THE BABY BONDING BOOK
FOR DADS

Building a Closer Connection with Your Baby

James di Properzio & Jennifer Margulis

Photographs by Christopher Briscoe

WILLOW CREEK PRESS

Published by Willow Creek Press
P.O. Box 147, Minocqua, Wisconsin 54548

*For information about custom editions, special sales, premium and
corporate purchases, please contact Jeremy Petrie at 800-850-9453 or
jpetrie@willowcreekpress.com.*

Editor/Design: Andrea Donner

Library of Congress Cataloging-in-Publication Data:

Di Properzio, James.
  The baby bonding book for dads : building a closer connection with
your baby / James di Properzio and Jennifer Margulis ; photographs by Christopher Briscoe.
     p. cm.
  ISBN 978-1-59543-589-7 (hardcover : alk. paper)
  1. Fathers. 2. Father and child. I. Margulis, Jennifer. II. Title.
  HQ756.D574 2008
  649'.122--dc22

                                    2007051412

Printed in Canada

For my father, James Propis

CONTENTS

PREFACE

My dad used to sit me on the bathroom counter while he shaved and brushed his teeth, finished dressing, and tied his tie. I did the same with my toddler. It would be before dawn and very quiet, and I would set our daughter on the side of the sink while I shaved, talking quietly to her.

Something about being alone together, trying not to wake the others, made it exciting and special for her. It didn't matter that I was busily getting ready; she was glad just to be there, and even the sense of purpose was fun for her, just as she still likes to come along on the most boring and mundane errands—to the post office, the DMV, even the dentist. When my daughter accompanies me, she doesn't act bored and impatient. The outing becomes more like an occasion, and I enjoy it more too.

One day, at the sink, she insisted on shaving me. She was just three. If not for the fact that I remember sitting on the sink to watch my dad shave, I wouldn't even have considered putting a razor into my toddler's hand and letting her at my throat. I showed her the motion (down, pick up, down—never sideways!—and don't press hard) and guided her hand through it a couple times. I told her how my grandfather, each morning before he went to elementary school, had gone upstairs to his own grandfather's room with a straight razor, soap, and brush, to shave him after he had gone blind in his old age. She looked totally absorbed by this, and held her hand steady, so I positioned her hand at the top of my cheek and let her try a stroke. She carefully removed a stripe of shaving cream from my cheek, without trimming a single whisker. We worked on the pressure a bit, and she did most of the flat, easy parts of my cheeks. My daughter was very proud to have been allowed this responsibility, and to have done something to care for me the way I normally took care of her. It was a bonding moment, which she has asked to repeat every few months since, and which I've carried on with her two younger siblings as they reached that age—without a single scratch.

Most men are like I was before my first child, having never even held a baby in our lives and with little or no experience taking care of kids. Women have nine months to get used to the idea that they're creating a new life. For men, it's a little slower to hit home. Of course we feel apprehensive about bonding and unsure how to interact with our offspring. I knew, though, that if I let my apprehension put me in the back seat in parenting, I would be taking a step back from one of the most important experiences of my life. I needed to take the initiative and create my own ways to bond with my child, right from the beginning.

It's hard to engage after work when you're tired and stressed, and part of the choice facing fathers is whether to play it safe, stay in that work mode and be hands-off at home, or to engage with our children, something for which we've had no practice, and makes us feel unsure of ourselves.

Bonding with a baby or small child is about the small moments that you spend together, looking at each other, talking, taking walks. It's not something that happens instantly. It's a relationship that grows over time. That's what this book is about: practical, everyday things to do to enjoy being with your children and forge the bond for both of you.

A lot of dads feel closer to older children, the ones who can catch a ball and enjoy a slice of pizza. But the bonding process starts in infancy, in hundreds of small ways. That's where we'll start—we'll get to ball and pizza later.

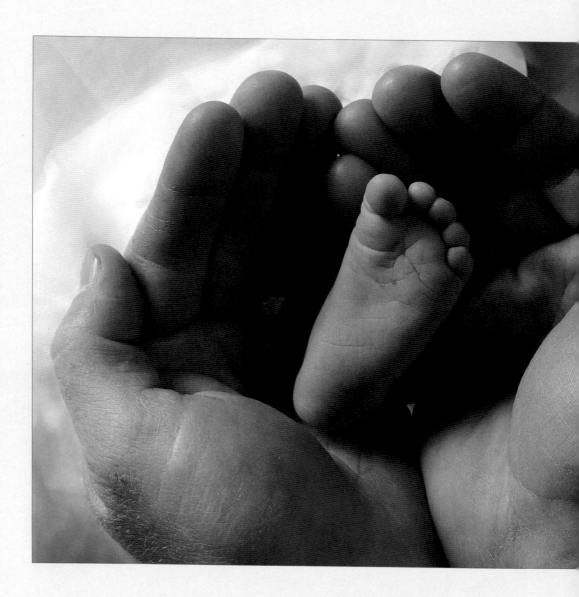

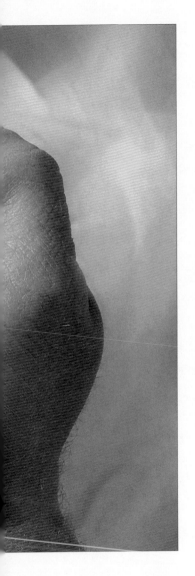

NEWBORN TIME

Unless your wife had a C-section, your new baby probably looks weird. He may be all scrunched up with a cone head like Bart Simpson, odd-looking skin that's been out of the sun and in amniotic fluid for nine months, and eyes that cross or look unfocused. He may have hemangioma (big red spots), swollen genitalia (due to maternal hormones), and a host of other strange features. This is probably not the best time to ask your wife if this or that is completely normal. Just take it in stride.

If you weren't all that comfortable with babies to begin with, you're really going to wonder what to do with a newborn. They're so light it doesn't feel like you're holding anything. Between that and the floppy neck, it's hard not to feel like you're going to break them. Don't worry; that never happens.

The first thing to do to get to know a newborn is to hold him as close to you as possible. Human infants need skin-to-skin contact and you can unbutton your shirt and scrunch the baby into it, like a kangaroo pouch, while your wife is sleeping in the hospital. If you recline and rest the newborn on your chest, head up toward your collar, he'll usually snuggle in very happily, and you can even read or watch TV—just don't sit up suddenly for the remote. The next thing to do is to smell his scalp (assuming the nurses haven't scrubbed it with antibiotic soap already). The smell of a new baby is warm and sweet and like nothing else, and it's actually a physiological part of bonding. The more you hold him and smell him, the quicker you and he will become buddies.

He probably has you at a disadvantage, since you know nothing about him, but he may well know your voice, which is audible through the womb. When you talk to him, he'll probably turn his face toward you to listen. Just being with him and doing little things to take care of him—changing his diaper, wrapping him like a burrito in a baby blanket—will help you bond. Every woman responds to childbirth differently and if your wife has had a difficult labor she may want you to take the lead with the baby at first; on the other hand, she may feel so possessive that she hardly lets you hold the kid for five minutes. Take the surge of love and protectiveness that you start to feel when you see and hold your new baby, add hormones, and you'll begin to understand your wife's urgent need to have the baby in her arms.

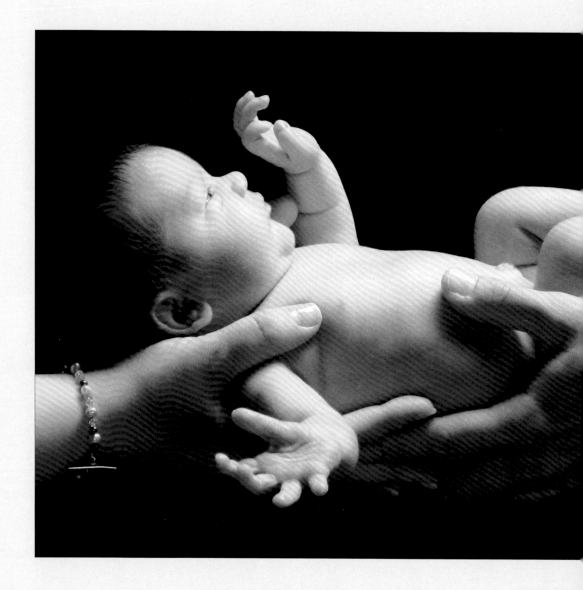

CARRYING

A mom named Kaitlyn was so afraid of dropping her newborn that she handed Aidan off to her husband as soon as he was born. More often, though, it's the guy who's afraid of dropping the baby. Whatever you might think looking at someone else's baby, yours isn't a slippery mound of Jell-O. Newborns are a little tricky; they usually have poor muscle tone and little ability to raise their heads. But once you have that pint-sized charge in your arms, her tiny head flopped onto your shoulder, her nearsighted eyes looking at a new world, you'll see that she's easier to hold—and harder to drop—than you thought. Even better, babies are patient little creatures who forgive your mistakes and don't hold a grudge if you smoosh their arm (unlike your wife.)

It looks easy to carry a newborn around in those bucket carriers that double as car seats, but the first time you lift one you'll be surprised by how awkward it is. Carrying the baby in the bucket is a good task for dads and it's convenient to set the seat down beside you. But while it may be convenient and trendy, it leads to infants spending a lot of time without human contact. If you want to bond with your baby and foster her growth and development you need to buck the current craze and hold the baby in your arms instead of in a car seat. When you kangaroo carry your baby in a front pack, you get to feel her tiny body next to yours, play with the toes that dangle by your sides, and gaze into her face (they face you for the first couple months, until their necks get stronger). She can feel your heart beat and you can feel hers. For the newborn, who has spent the last several months touched on all sides (and with constant company), touch is everything. For the dad who wants to bond with his baby, that closeness is important.

Maybe you read the story about the dad who dropped the baby on her head in the subway? The good news is that even if you do drop your baby, chances are she'll be fine (whether *you* recover or not is another story). "Their bones are supple, like green branches," a doctor said when I fell hard on the snow with my daughter in my arms, "they're made to bounce."

And once you get over the apprehension, nothing will warm your heart like the feel of your very own child in your arms.

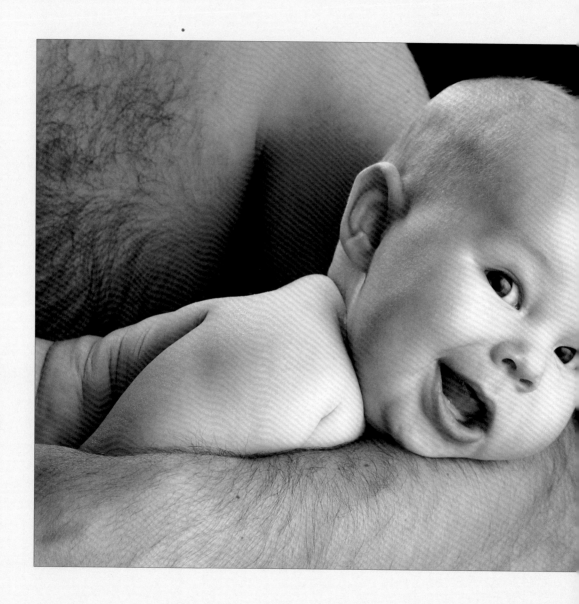

SKIN TO SKIN

You've seen the poster: a black-and-white photo of a buff, bare-chested guy, cradling a cute newborn in his birthday suit. We doubt that man is actually the father of that child (what father of a newborn has the time to get his chest waxed?), but aside from being the literal poster child for being an involved dad, it shows the power of skin-to-skin touch with your baby so clearly you can feel it.

Newborns have a physiological reaction to direct touch—which means their bare skin on yours, not through a layer of cloth—it stimulates their endocrine system to produce growth hormones and reduce stress hormones, helps them sleep better, and promotes weight gain. Studies of infants with more or less time spent skin-to-skin have shown that their growth is affected by the time they spend in direct skin contact with adults. Babies in orphanages often fail to thrive because of the total lack of skin-to-skin touch. Holding your kids isn't just about comfort—their bodies need it.

You need it, too. Dads don't give birth or nurse, and we come into less direct contact with the baby. But really bonding to a child, not just as a responsibility but as someone you love, isn't an intellectual thing; it's physical, and it involves time, presence, and touch.

There's something else here: let's face it, if you grew up like me as an American man without a lot of contact with kids, you may have found yourself as an adult with the idea that you would probably have kids at some point, but without the strong feeling that you really wanted them right now that many women have. So you may be anticipating having a baby with a big worry: will I really bond with this child? Since when is "Dad" part of who I am?

Don't be squeamish: take off your shirt, pick your baby up in his just his diaper, and hold him. The skin-to-skin effect will work on you, too. You're going to feel

his skin against yours, smell his smell, and know that
you're really holding your baby. He's going to feel like
yours. Which he is. For the rest of your life.

And you're going to look like that guy in the
poster—in your baby's eyes anyway.

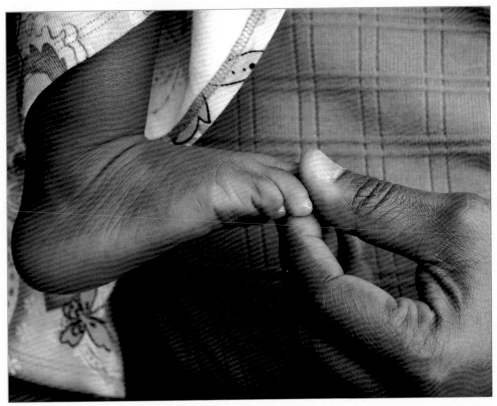

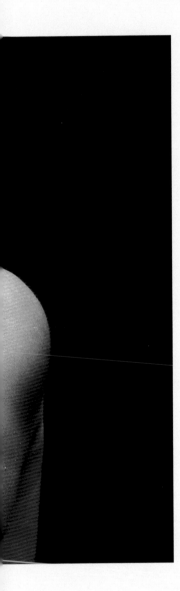

COMFORTING

If you have a baby prone to cry, your wife has already spent hundreds of dollars on advice books and if you leaf through them you'll see they all say the same thing: Check that the baby isn't being poked by a pin, check that the baby isn't too cold—useful stuff like that to solve the problem that your kid won't stop fussing and you and the mother are both going out of your mind. (No wonder fathers don't read parenting books.)

Here's the truth: babies cry. If you've got one, there is going to be some crying. Your baby will cry sometimes even if he doesn't have a wet diaper (if you use synthetic diapers you can't even tell when it's wet), and isn't hungry, or whatever. In the first three months the human brain is growing exponentially and that's a lot of neuron firing that can lead—in some infants at least—to a lot of crying. Earplugs and a sense of humor help. So does a clean pinky with a closely cut fingernail upside down in the baby's mouth (in fact, "the finger" is such an effective remedy that one mother we know is apt to scream to her husband: "She's crying! Can you please go give her the finger!"). But even if nothing is helping, being there with your baby while he's fussing is a way for you to bond.

It's a simple task and not one to dread. You're keeping the baby company as he goes through a stage, and showing both of you that you care for him. The baby's going to be doing some crying, and your comforting him is the first big bonding experience that will make him feel taken care of by you. There's nothing else you can do, so you may as well take it in stride. In a soothing voice you can crack stupid jokes at your fussy baby's expense, you can watch TV while jiggling the little screamer (knee bends sometimes help), or take him outside and get sympathetic looks from childless women who will be eager to help. You can also use noise-isolating earphones with your mp3 player and listen to whatever you want. (You'll be amazed at how you feel your stress level go down when you can comfort an infant without having to hear the crying.)

It's hard to realize when you're in the thick of crying jags, but they'll be over very soon—there's nothing you need to do but get through it.

DIAPERING

"I'll never change a smelly diaper," uncle Julius said with absolute certainty before having children. Still, when his dogs vomit all over the floor he cleans up the mess without flinching. It's funny what people choose to be all squeamish about.

Muhammad Ali said while his wife was expecting their first child that he wouldn't change diapers either, and that it was women's work. But his wife later said that without anyone prodding him, or even knowing about it, the Greatest decided to teach himself to change diapers anyway, because he wanted to take care of his kid.

If your wife is breastfeeding, your newborn's poop will look sort of like runny scrambled eggs and it will actually have a sweetish smell, like apricots. We're not making this up. The real challenge doesn't come until your baby transitions to solid food and then things get really interesting. But by then you'll be a diaper-changing pro. My trick was to learn to do it so efficiently that it was done in seconds, often leaving my wife stunnned that the kid was diapered already.

So how do you do it? Don't be surprised if you need to call in reinforcements the first few times you try to change a diaper. The hospital nurses may be able to change a diaper with regimented efficiency but those floppy newborns wiggle a lot and there's something a bit daunting about the many steps involved. First survey the damage. Chances are it's not only in her diaper but goes halfway up her back as well. Say, "Good job!" (It becomes funnier every time.)

Then find a clean surface to lay your baby on—a safe one the baby can't roll off. Changing tables are fine but the bed, the floor, the couch, even a chair, all work just as well. On the go, I use the car's back hatch. Just be sure to lay a changing pad or towel under the baby. Before you put her down, collect what you need: a clean diaper, a soft cloth and a bottle of water (or baby wipes), and a clean outfit.

Next step: wrestle her out of her clothes. Newborns can't cooperate with this, and a lot of baby clothing isn't well designed to let you get the arms and legs out. When the clothes are smeared with yellow goo, getting them off without smearing it over her head becomes like ju-jitsu. It's a good idea to talk to the baby and distract her so she doesn't fuss: talk about your day, the Red Sox, or tell her how much better she'll feel once she's clean. Or if things get particularly funky, sing *"She's a very stinky girl,"* to the tune of "She's a very kinky girl." Once the offending garments are removed, clean her up with the wipes or the water and washcloth. The stuff gets into hard-to-find places so clean everywhere (on boys, lift up the penis to wipe down the folds of the scrotum; on girls, get in between the labia). No scowling or complaining allowed during this process. You are bonding.

DRESSING
TO IMPRESS

Dressing a baby with a floppy head and poor muscle tone is a tricky business. You might make the mistake Patrick made and put your son's overalls on backwards. Who cares, right? But the lady who just gave birth to your precious offspring, the same one who has been getting weepy over long-distance phone commercials, might not feel the same way about your honest mistake. She may even start ranting about dividing up assets. Patrick's wife did. Over a pair of overalls. (Then she went on Prozac.)

Issues of where the tags go (in the back) aside, getting baby dressed is a good opportunity to have some fun. Your wife may spend more time examining her waistline in the mirror than you do, but who doesn't like looking sharp? You'll feel a sense of accomplishment if you manage to get the baby dressed in anything at all, and you might take even more pride in your new Mini Me if you pick out something snazzy for him to wear.

Talk to the baby as you dress him, tell him what you're doing—he may not understand it now, but he'll enjoy the sound of your voice. Hold up the outfit in front of your face and play peek-a-boo with it. Rub your face against the soft skin on your baby's exposed belly and let him grab your hair and tug. And then play "Where's Your Hand?," a time-tested favorite game for babies and kids of all ages. Since getting a baby's arm into a sleeve is harder than stuffing a sausage casing, you'll want to play this game anyway to keep yourself from going insane. Start stuffing (gently) said floppy arm. Ask the baby, "Where's your hand?" and look around confused. Keep asking (this may take a while) until you manage to work the arm into the sleeve and pop the hand out the other end. "There it is!" you cry in genuine surprise. The older the baby, the more he'll enjoy this game.

If you aren't heading out the door, when he's finally

dressed, snap a few pictures (or better yet, get your wife to take them of both of you). In thirty seconds the little bugger is guaranteed to have an explosive poop all over the outfit it took you thirty minutes to get on him.

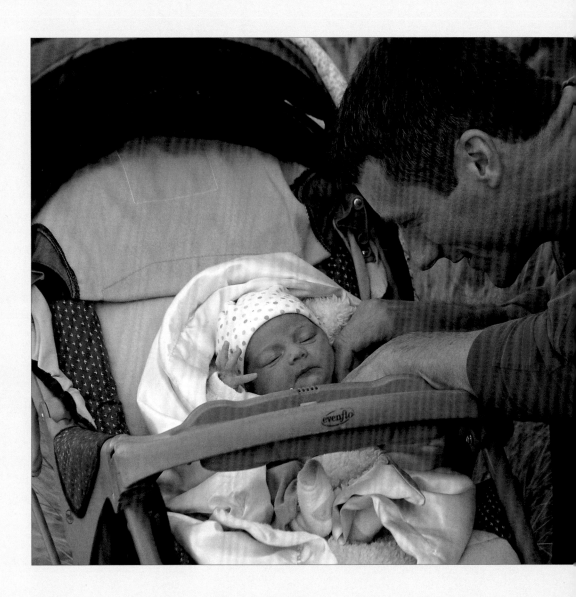

GOING PLACES

"He's so adorable!" a group of women coo in your direction when you take your baby out for a stroll. You don't have to look twice to see who they're talking about: you, of course.

Actually, they're admiring your new baby. But like father, like son or daughter, right? And one of the best perks about being a hands-on dad is that your offspring will attract all sorts of other babes to you.

Did you ever notice that, when your wife was pregnant, random women would stop her on the street and share intimate details of their private anatomy? Becoming a mother is like becoming part of a club neither of you ever knew existed. Becoming a father is like that too, but since your wife being pregnant doesn't show on you (we're not counting that 15 pounds of sympathy weight you gained), the transformation takes place for fathers after the baby's born. You suddenly have something in common with anyone with a baby close to the same age as yours, you can tap into the seemingly vast knowledge of fathers with older children, and serve as the wise guide to expectant dads.

A friend of ours complained for more than a year that he couldn't wait for his daughter to get bigger, so that they could go places instead of staying around the house. He was worried about interrupting her nap, changing a diaper far from the changing table, or having the baby fuss. Maybe it takes having more than one kid to figure this out but, guys, little babies don't get more portable. They're made to take with you! They're light, small, and easily carried, and for the most part they just look around, grunt, and sleep. Even babies prone to crying tend to be quieter and more alert when they're on the go. Better still, your baby's like a goodwill ambassador—everybody's impressed when they see a dad solo with a baby. Bring a snack in a bottle and some diapers and you're set for hours (and here's a tip: you don't need a changing table, just a bathroom sink and some paper towels, when the inevitable happens). When they're really small you can take them where *you* want to go— the art museum, the Red Sox game, the coffee house. (Enjoy it now. This will change.)

Running errands, going downtown, taking a hike, are all a little more festive with a baby along. Our second daughter was born in a cold, snowy New England winter, and from her first week liked nothing better than being taken for a walk into town, strapped under my coat. We'd hit the deli, the post office, and the bookstore, and when I came home and tried to take my coat off, she'd cry in protest. She didn't give us the choice of staying around the house.

What's to wait for? The baby's along for the ride in your life, not vice-versa, and they prefer it that way. Some things change: poker and extreme sports might not be appropriate bonding activities, yet. But if you're happy, getting out and doing things, your sidekick will be too. The moral of the story: take your new accoutrement out with you often, whether exercising or getting your hair cut.

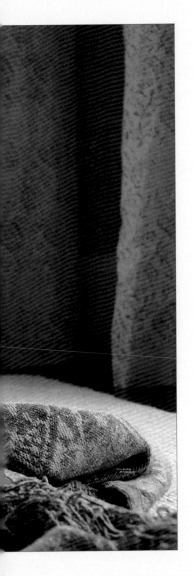

FACE TIME

This is what it's all about: spending time face-to-face with your baby. Babies' brains are wired to look for faces and learn to recognize and bond to them—even before they can fully focus their eyes. So taking the time to get up close and look at this little creature is one of the most important things you can do in the first year. You don't need to have an agenda, or be amusing—just be there. Talking's good, and if you run out of stuff to say to a baby, then talk to the kid she'll turn into in a few years (who will by then understand English), or even just to yourself. If you're the quiet type, you don't have to talk. Just looking at your baby is the first step to face time bonding.

Anything you do with your face is interesting, too. Pretend to look surprised, wiggle your ears. Blow little puffs of air into the baby's face and then laugh or make surprised noises—even gorillas play this game with their young—and your baby will either laugh or frown. This is your first chance to let go of your staid, grown-up demeanor and be silly, because nobody wants to be like the really serious, boring old dads some of your friends had when you were a kid. Maybe you don't feel like a cool dad yet, but when you were a kid, like every kid, you knew in your heart that you weren't going to be a strict/boring/old-fashioned/whatever like your dad. This is prime practice time, because babies are like dogs: they don't care what you do so much, as long as you're paying attention to them.

Face time can be tactile time, too. Even before babies' nervous systems can control their hands, they still like to touch things, people, liquids, anything. Take your baby's hands and put them on your face, she'll like the feel of your cheek, whether it's scratchy or smooth. When my daughter could reach out and hold on, I played a game with her by letting her grab my ears and nose and pull them—harmless to you and hilarious to an infant.

Some babies have a low attention threshold and if she turns her face to the side she's probably telling you she's had enough, and that your big bonding moment might be over for the time being. The more you look at her the more you'll learn to read her signals (and to appreciate the fact that she inherited your chin).

BED TIME

If you work regular daytime hours, you might only see your baby (and your disheveled wife who's home for a few months of maternity leave and more than happy to pass the kid, like a football, to you the minute you walk in the door) around bedtime. If you have an easy baby as a newborn his bedtime will consist of a diaper change, some late night snacking on the one menu item (milk or formula), and a little fussing before falling asleep sitting up in the crook of your arm as you surf the internet and watch TV at the same time. If you have a "livelier" baby, shall we say, his bedtime ritual may involve you pacing the house in a figure eight for several hours while he wails as if being stuck by needles. You wonder how you'll survive going to work in the morning but feel good about the fact that your very tired wife is getting a short nap between feedings. Hey, we never said this baby bonding would be easy.

But as the baby grows older, the rituals of bedtime become more important and more established. Even a baby who is just a few months old can learn to recognize that the sound of water means a bath before bed and you might notice your little offspring flailing his arms in happy anticipation. Bedtime rituals become part of a child's feelings of home and comfort, and it's important to establish a ritual that's comforting for both of you and a time to bond (expect bedtime to take up to an hour but don't get your child hooked on anything that takes a really *l-o-n-g* time because—as you'll find when they grow—they'll be wanting to listen to that same sleepy tape or that same sleepy story about Charlie the Elephant over and over and over again). Even if your kids spend most of their day with other caregivers or teachers, their parents, who are there at home and putting them to bed, are still the cornerstone of their lives. Bedtime is a time for both of you to unwind together and a time for dads to comfort and actively take care of their kids. By planning the stages of bedtime, and doing them always at the same time, you also get your baby psychologically ready to sleep.

The basic sequence is something like: bathing, pajamas, toothbrushing, books, lullaby/story, tucking in, hugs and a kiss goodnight. Some of these things will drop in and out of importance over time (newborns don't have teeth to brush), but you should keep the same framework. Even when your newborn can't focus her eyes, start reading books at bedtime. The short, colorful picture books appropriate for this age don't take long to read; she'll probably like looking at the colors, and she can lie back on your chest and listen to the sound of your voice. Early habits of togetherness can last a lifetime. Start bedtime early enough so you don't have to hurry. For your baby this becomes a time of undivided attention from you, a time to feel like her world is ordered and caring.

FOOD TIME

One of the mysterious baby activities many dads aren't looking forward to is feeding them. It's messy, domestic, suspiciously close to cooking, and possibly outright dangerous. What if he chokes? Having never so much as touched a baby before my first child was born, I was happy to agree with my wife that it would be breast milk only for the first year.

Until she went to work a few weeks later. Then I was not only responsible for feeding the baby, I was alone in the house—no backup! She would pump, we decided, and I would feed the baby breast milk, coming as close as a man gets to nursing.

Before she left for work we had to figure out the

breast pump. Despite the innocuous black briefcase it was housed in, there were enough moving parts to send my wife into a postpartum fit of tears, so I figured out how to assemble and work it and then explained it to her. But even if your wife is exclusively breastfeeding and not pumping, you can get involved in nursing the baby too. Be on hand to bring her a glass of water (don't wait until she asks for one) and also make sure she has some food in a bowl by her favorite nursing place. Nursing women are often ravenous, and ravenous women are grumpy, so make sure she's eating. The more you bond with your wife, the more bonded you'll be to the little nursling you created together. If you're bottle-feeding your baby, you can be the one to give the bottles.

The good news about bottles is that they're easier than the real deal, so technical difficulties are rare. And it turns out that it's a wonderful thing to have a baby drinking a bottle in your arms, as peaceful as they get, looking up into your face contentedly and with mild interest. This was one of the most bonding experiences I had, when I felt as content and happy as my daughter looked.

Later on there will be real food, which is potentially even more fun. (All of my kids are now trained to catch food I throw into their mouths from across the table, just like the Blues Brothers.) The American Academy of Pediatrics recommendation is to introduce solids when your baby is between four and six months old. If your child inherited your impatience genes, he may be grabbing food off the table and stuffing it into his mouth as soon as he can sit on your lap (one dad we know calls the mouth a third hand). If he's on a slower train, he'll have no interest whatsoever in solids until he's close to one. It's normal for kids to drink nothing but milk for a full year, so whatever works for your baby is what you should follow. Still, watching a baby eat solids for the first time is an experience you don't want to miss. It's not really about nourishment—it's more like a whole body and mind encounter.

You can be adventurous and try something mushy, like avocado, banana, or boiled and mashed yam as a first food. Whatever you give him, the baby's look of surprise will crack you up, as will his pleasure at the texture and feel of the food in his mouth (though it's just as likely to end up all over your shirt as in his stomach). Snap a picture and enjoy him enjoying it.

BONDING
IN NATURE

While it may be true that many fathers, given the choice, would rather plop down on the couch with Baby over one shoulder, a drink in one hand, and a movie on TV than go hiking, the majority of babies would rather you take them outside. Now. No matter the weather.

When our second born was a temperamental infant, the fussing stopped the instant we stepped outside. Being surrounded by interesting sights and smells and sounds calmed her at once, and as soon as we stepped back in over the threshold, she'd start fussing again. Her less temperamental siblings also loved being outside, whether they were being hiked up a mountain, ridden in a baby seat on the back of a bicycle, or walked in the woods.

Spending time outdoors with your baby is as grounding for you as it is for the baby. Studies suggest that humans, who have spent the vast majority of our evolutionary history in hunter-gatherer groups that have direct daily contact with nature, feel less stress and more well being when we are outside. Some men experience angst when they become fathers, fearing that their old lives are over and their new lives involve nothing but spit-up cloths and dirty diapers. Taking a baby with you on your favorite outdoor activity (our friend Peter used to fly fish with his son in a back carrier) is also a way to bridge the gap between your old daring life and your new responsible one.

Like to bike? In Africa and other places around the world, it's common to see an infant strapped to his mother's back while she rides a bicycle, or a one-year-old sitting on the back bike rack in front of a sibling, while his father cycles at top speed. In America we're a little more safety conscious and any bike contraption you buy to haul your baby will come with a specific set of warnings about when the baby's ready to go in it. The official word is usually at about one year of age, when they can sit up unaided and have strong enough neck muscles to wear a helmet. A bike enthusiast, I started tooling around town and out on the bike path with my kids well before their first birthdays. But don't tell anyone.

Those shared experiences outside become your family's history and make up your kid's memories of his childhood. I still remember when my parents had one of those clunky old-fashioned bike seats with a metal pipe frame and red-and-black checked vinyl cushions. I would sit behind my dad and—according to him—pat his back, pull his shirt, and chatter nonstop the whole time he was riding. The part I remember is bicycling up the hill to Main Street, past the big waterfall on a stream that connected my two favorite parks, through the little downtown and under a railroad bridge. I knew when I saw the black metal trestles overhead that we were almost at the ice cream store. My dad would stand over the frame to stabilize it while we ate our ice cream, facing backward toward me in my seat.

The shared experience of being outdoors together will make you feel closer to your baby. And the smile of exultation on his face as he feels the wind on his cheeks and sees the world go by from a different perspective is one you will never forget.

SNOOZING

Newborns do a lot of is napping. Their body clock isn't adjusted to a day-and-night cycle, so they stay awake for a couple hours, then nap for a little while, all day long—and often all night, too. Unless, that is, you have a screamer who only cries and nurses and never seems to nap. In that case, skip this chapter because you're too tired to read anyway.

Every parenting book you read will tell your wife to "nap while the baby is napping." Ha! Real parents know that most of the time naps are a good opportunity to get things done, and women often find themselves unable to settle down for the time the baby is sleeping. While your wife jumps up to check email, you can use the time to bond. Believe it or not, naps are one of the best ways for you to soak up some time with your newborn, when your baby isn't making any needs or demands on you (or your wife). Even the gruffest guy, if he's handed a sleeping baby, automatically holds it gently, talks quietly, and can't help but feel pretty charmed by the little person sleeping on him. You don't have to do anything—just hold them.

When your baby goes to sleep while you're holding her (try picking her up when she looks just about to), sit down in a comfortable chair or on your bed and just look. Listen to her breathing. Feel the trust and total relaxation of the tiny person in your arms, who is totally secure there. Your baby knows you're there. And you can sit and soak it up, let go of some of your daily worries, and feel some of that relaxation yourself.

You might even feel so relaxed you doze off too, sometimes, with your baby sleeping on your chest. Napping together counts as bonding, and that much needed snooze with your baby will help you gear up for what may be another long night.

BABY WRESTLING

One thing most moms don't do with kids is play vigorously—or as they call it, "roughly." But babies are very physical; they love touch and cuddles (the part your wife's good at), and they also love motion. If your wife looks at you roughhousing with the baby disapprovingly, explain to her that movement actually stimulates a baby's vestibular system, the part of the brain that perceives movement and balance, and that studies of very small children have shown that when the vestibular system is stimulated with motion, infants develop reflexes and gross motor skills more easily and quickly. This means that when you carry, rock, or swing your baby, the movement actually helps foster brain development and coordination.

So try putting your palm on the your baby's belly and lifting her as high as you can in the air. She gets a fascinating new perspective, plus a new sensation that will often stop low-grade crying and fussing. Just make sure you're smiling into her face, so she knows the new perspective is a good one to have—a lot of how babies decide whether something is okay or worth a good cry depends on how you are reacting. And if your baby doesn't like to free float, try something else.

One of my kids' favorite things, of which their mother does not approve, is baby wrestling. Lie on your back on the bed with the baby on your chest and wrap your arms all the way around her so that they secure her in place while also forming a frame around her. Then say, "Baby wrestling! Baby wrestling! Baby wrestling!" and roll onto your side (being careful not to let the little arms and legs flop out under your heavy torso) and over until you are supported on your elbows, then continue over onto your back again so the baby's pinned you. Then say dramatically, "Oh, the baby's got me down!" After a few more rolls and a valiant struggle, the dad ends up on his back and says, "One, two, three!" The baby always wins, in the end, which seems an apt metaphor for life with babies.

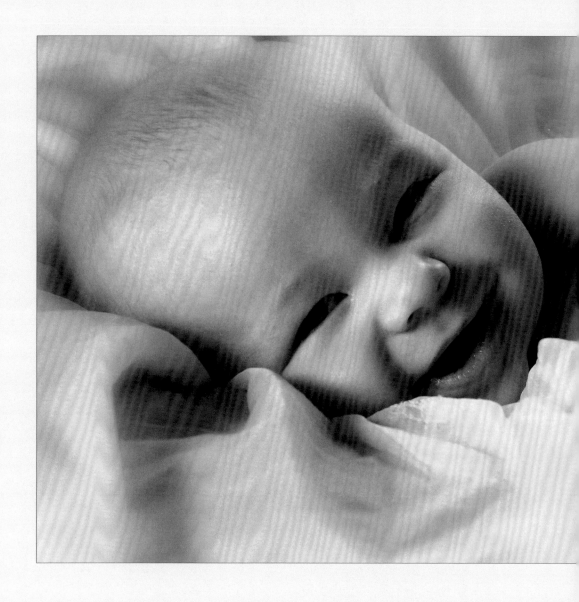

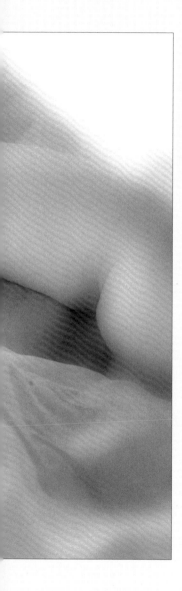

SINGING

You may sing like Pavarotti (in shower-stall acoustics) or have less sense of rhythm than Steve Martin in *The Jerk*; it doesn't matter—singing to children has a powerful effect, which has nothing to do with the quality of your voice. In fact, your baby loves to hear your voice; he's been hearing it in utero for the nine months when you were talking to your wife while she was pregnant, and he will turn his face toward the sound of your voice to show he recognizes it after he is born. Babies prefer your homey crooning to a trained opera voice any day of the week. Think Sinatra, Bing Crosby—think Dino! Newborns dig the Rat Pack; nobody can feel self-conscious singing such mellow, corny stuff, and anybody can sing as well as

Dino. If you feel self-conscious about singing or find your ability to hold a tune laughable, do it anyway and go ahead and laugh—the baby won't hear anything wrong with your voice, but will enjoy your laughter all the same. (They don't become music critics until their teens.)

You don't have to sing those maddening Raffi songs someone bought your wife for the baby shower. Lullabies are sometimes nice to soothe a fussy baby but you should sing whatever you like. Do your best karaoke number, or practice to be the next American Idol—your infant will be your biggest fan. I started my kids out with Lead-belly's 'Goodnight Irene' (*"Stop ramblin', stop your gamblin'...."*), which is set to a lullaby tune, despite the fact that in the end the narrator heads off to jump in the river. I didn't even bother to change the words until they were old enough to understand the lyrics. It's still one of their favorites, requested night after night, though now it starts, *"I'm feelin' sleepy, my darlin'; looks like you're sleepy, too...."* The refrain stays.

Personalizing songs by inserting your baby's name is another nice way to sing, or try making up silly lyrics about your baby to a familiar tune. This one goes to *Baa Baa Black Sheep*: *"Hannah Banana have you any tears?*

Yes Daddy yes Daddy running in my ears. One for my mommy and one for my dad, and one for the little girl in case she gets sad." Papa's singing is not only deeply comforting to babies, it's also a way to inspire your child to have a lifetime love for music. When your baby's a little older you'll be doing duets.

Christopher Briscoe

BOOK TIME

It's never too early to read to your baby. Your first reaction might be, "Isn't reading for later, once my child begins to read... or at least talk?" Babies learn to understand language before they can talk and the more they hear the faster they learn. Reading not only gets you talking, but it gets you to stay there, relaxed and engaged with the baby, for a period of time.

Most babies are captivated by the pictures in a book, and by the sound of your voice, and will sit still and listen for a few minutes. This is what developmental specialists call "quiet alert time," which is prime time for learning, when they are neither active nor sleepy, with their brains fully engaged. In the first few weeks and months, their brains are doing a lot of just soaking up images, learning what to make of the fascinating visual stimuli that come their way, as well as the sounds of language.

A more active baby will gladly take her pudgy hand and try to bat the book while you read. As mentioned earlier, babies are also hardwired to particularly respond to faces—anything shaped like a face—and picture books tend to have lots of faces in them. Your words may not make sense to them, but at the early stages, they are learning to recognize the sounds that make up language—as well as the rhythms of speech and the nuances of your tone of voice. Long before they understand the words, they'll be able to follow the gist of a story through the pictures and the tone of your voice, particularly if you read slowly and with drama.

Just leaning back with you, on your lap or chest, or with your arm around them, and listening to you, gives a baby the feeling of safety and care that is essential to bonding. And you'll also be doing one of the most important things you can for your child's future achievement: instilling the habit of reading, as a daily activity, right from the beginning. When your Mini-Me is really little you can also read a book to yourself while she's gnawing on teething toes, or read your book aloud to her. One of the surest ways to teach kids to do something is to model it, to let them see you doing it, whether smoking or reading. Pick reading.

BABY AEROBICS

A floppy newborn who can't lift her head or control her limbs may not seem like a candidate for exercise, but she is: exercising baby (most of which she'll passively do herself) is exactly how she'll grow stronger and learn to coordinate movements. Parents today tend to keep their newborns in bucket-seat carriers, bouncy chairs, and battery-operated swings much of the time, which not only deprives them of needed human contact, but prevents them from moving and developing their muscles.

Passive exercise is one of the first ways for the baby to develop balance, coordination, and muscle tone. When you're carrying the baby and moving, the baby is not a floppy dead weight; they begin to hang on, they conform to your body, and they stabilize themselves (by contrast, imagine holding something truly floppy, like a large freezer bag half-full of water). Even in the first few days after birth, their muscles will try to hold them in a partial fetal position, arms and legs bent, and they will resist being stretched out to full length, as they do when the doctors measure them and assess neonatal (newborn) muscle tone.

You'll notice that your baby, whether you are holding her or she's lying down, is often moving: squirming her legs, flailing her little arms. In a word, exercising. But while she can and will do this exercise herself, doing baby sit-ups and baby gymnastics with her is fun for dads and good for babies. For baby sit-ups, lie your baby on your lap with her feet against your stomach and her head on your knees, and let her grasp your thumbs while you grasp her forearms. Pull her gently up by the arms until she is in a sitting position. She'll be shocked—her world view has changed!

Here's how we do baby gymnastics: Lie the baby on her back and hold onto her legs; alternate pumping them and tell her she is "running, running, running." Then bicycle her legs and tell her she is "bicycling to work, bicycling home again." Then push her leg gently to her head or to the opposite arm and say "One, two, one two," as if you are counting the number of leg presses she's doing. Then grab both legs and pull them off the ground and say, "Hoppy frog, hoppy frog, gymnastics." Maybe it's the singsong voice, maybe the pure absurdity of movement, or maybe the sheer joy of exercise but I've never met a baby who didn't love to work out in this way.

You may be surprised at how early you get a strong response of pushing or kicking downward from the baby—she's using the muscles that will be in play when she starts walking later on. If you stand a baby as young as two months old in your lap she might tense her legs. She's exercising! Some cultures that heavily emphasize physical play to encourage infant development, like hunter-gatherers in Africa, get their infants sitting, crawling, and walking much earlier than we do, simply because they lack strollers and carriers, and they play by helping the baby simulate these actions—it works!

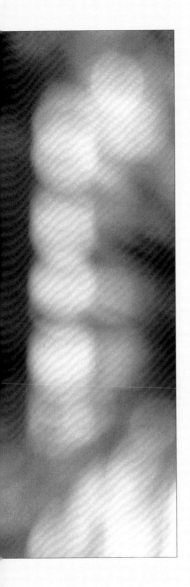

BALL TIME

A little early for hardball or to sign up for Little League maybe, but that doesn't mean you can't start them on the basics. Our friend's baby Asher used to hold onto what his mom called a "nipple ball" (a plastic contraption with little protrusions all over it) like he would never relinquish it. Babies love balls—not for sports, just for the sheer wonder of a sphere. Very early on they like looking at balls, balloons, and stuffed-animal-style balls; soccer balls are good too, because a baby's eyes pick up on the high contrast between black and white. Once they can grasp, they like soft-stuffed balls, and you can play little games of holding them out and pulling them back, tug-of-war, and gently tickling their noses or tummies with the ball. They'll spend a lot of time squeezing the balls, too. As you hold a ball out to your child to grab, you're not just bonding with the baby and offering him a toy, you're teaching him a skill set that will come in handy later. More than just fun, your baby's actually hard at work on eye-hand coordination.

Here's a baby ball game that you won't read about in any parenting magazine: Tie a balloon on a very short string either to the baby's wrist or to something very close (like a crib bar at eye level), so the baby's within flailing range. You'll watch your child literally become shocked with the delight of bonking the balloon as he flails his hands up and down at eye-popping speed trying to fathom the essence of it, watching it move, and listening to the noise it makes. However you do it, don't give them enough string to choke themselves and make sure they don't pop the balloon (choking hazard potential).

Once the tyke can sit up, you can sit across from him, feet-to-feet with your legs in the same sort of V, and roll the ball. He'll get the idea pretty quickly that he can just hit at it and get it rolling back to you. If you have a collector who wants to keep all the balls you roll his way, stock up before sitting down, and crumple up some used printer paper from the recycling bin to keep the game going longer. Playing ball is the first sport you can do with your baby, and has a way of engaging both your interest and the baby's. (Although not for all that long; when your baby gets bored, looks away, or starts to fuss, the ball playing's over.) Maybe you'd rather be watching Tivo but remember, you're laying the foundation for later sports skills, which start developing from here.

PICTURE TIME

If you're the one in the house who takes the pictures, you'll soon find that there are lots of pictures of the baby, and of the baby and your wife, but almost none of the baby and you. This is often the dad's place: looking in on the action, wanting to record it all, but not in the picture. But to bond with your baby you need to get into the frame, so to speak. My grandfather took hundreds of hours of Super-8 movies of the family—but he's not in any of them, because nobody else knew how to use the camera! It's a bit misleading: the pictures without you in them are indirect proof that you were there, but of course everybody also wants to see you with the baby— especially you and the baby—once he grows up.

Digital video cameras make taking video of yourself fun and easy—you flip the fold-out view screen around, and you can see when you're in the frame. For the first few months, the baby won't know the camera's there and will go ahead and do his thing—drooling, passing gas, spitting up—with happy oblivion. Later, kids like it once they can recognize themselves, and just before they learn to recognize themselves they go through a period of staring wide-eyed at themselves on the little screen, perfectly still, mouths agape. While not very action-oriented, this stage is pretty funny for as long as it lasts. Once you're set up, forget the camera and just go ahead and play. Tell the baby what game you're going to play, make funny faces and noises, and otherwise loosen up and make a fool of yourself. I have an audiocassette of my dad trying to teach me a song—at the age of ten months—that's hilarious to listen to even now, and my kids love it.

Don't wait for a special occasion to whip out a camera—record everyday life. Babies change so much in the first several months that every stage goes at fast forward speed, and if you look at the footage a couple of months later, you'll already be amazed at how different and grown-up your little one seems. At the end of the first year, you'll have a child very different from a newborn, and it's good to see the stages as they happen. The first year as a parent is like the first year of college: one of the fullest years of your life, but also one of the fastest to go by, leaving everything different.

TALKING

Newborns aren't big conversationalists, but they're often the most rapt listeners you've ever had. Their brains are learning your language just by hearing it for a matter of months, and well before their first birthday, they will understand you and may start to answer. But they won't learn to converse if they aren't exposed to a constant stream of language. Your most boring talk about work, or enthusiastic talk about a band they've never seen, is as fascinating to them as a kaleidoscope. They're taking in the sheer variety and music of your words, and working on it like codebreakers. When my wife and I would take our daughter for a walk in the stroller while we got a chance to catch up with each other, the baby would stare at me open-mouthed the whole time I talked, as if I were singing Puccini while juggling burning torches and doing the macarena.

Talking to your baby is also a way to help your baby recognize you and bond to the sound of your voice. And you've probably already started that part—in the last several weeks before birth, they can hear things in utero, not distinctly but probably about like you can hear underwater. So they already know the voice of their mother and likely their father too, who's been talking to their mother at close range every day. Maybe my daughter's amazement was just to find out that I actually spoke words, and no longer sounded like Charlie Brown's teacher, "Mwah-ma-wa mwah-meh."

As much as you talk, pause and listen too. Give her space to contribute to the dialogue. Your silence invites your baby to respond. Even though she sounds like she's just babbling, remember that one day you'll be talking about the stock market and the president's latest policies, and that you're setting up a relationship that will ensure you have father-to-daughter or father-to-son talks for the rest of your life.

WRITING TO
YOUR BABY

Maybe you hate writing. Maybe you failed English and have never recovered. Or maybe you like to write long emails, letters, journal entries, and such. It doesn't matter whether you consider yourself a writer or not; once you have a baby, you'll have a lot to tell him and writing as much as you can to your child is a good way for you to feel close to him, before he's old enough to take to the park to play catch. It doesn't matter if you write him two pages once a year, a letter on his birthday, or a diary of 200 pages like Sgt. Charles Monroe King, an American soldier who died in Iraq and left a written legacy to his infant son. It's not the quantity or the quantity, it's the act of writing itself (and then when he's a teenager and starts accusing you of not caring, you have the evidence, albeit spotty, to prove him wrong.)

A family journal that includes written entries and photographs and baby paraphernalia is a good place to write to your baby, but if you'd rather leave the scrapbooking to your wife, you can write down your thoughts in a computer file or on odd bits of paper. Anything goes. You can tell your baby things you want him to know about you and your family, and you can tell him about himself as he grows and matures, and about the things you do together. Here's an example from before our oldest daughter was born. (Now we have three journals, one for each child. They get written in infrequently, but we don't let that stop us from keeping them.)

Last night while your mother was sleeping I put my arm around her and spread my hand over her bulging belly. I'd felt what I thought were little movements before, but while she slept soundly, breathing deep and even, totally relaxed, I felt a sharp and vigorous movement under my fingers. I became very alert, and real-

ized it had been nothing she ever could have
done. A few heartbeats later my palm was lifted
up from the plane of my fingers by a pronounced
little bulge like an egg being pressed outward
from under her skin. Many equally firm kicks
and punches followed like a soccer match in her
womb. She was sleeping; you and I were both
wide awake.

EPILOGUE

The early days with a new baby sometimes seem endless. Trying to juggle work, home, diapers, your marriage—not to mention all the other stresses that life sends—can be overwhelming, and a lot of dads would rather go golfing on the weekends than hang out with a tiny baby. When you're bonding with a baby you don't do much that can be quantified or tallied. You smile, you interact, you talk, you be. Maybe you'll sit and read a book with your baby flopped over your shoulder, or maybe you'll shake a rattle in front of him, letting him bat at it with disjointed hand movements, until he looks bored and turns away. But before you know it your baby will be a toddler and then a preschooler and then a bonafide kid.

I sat next to an older guy on a plane once who (after the flight was delayed and the stewardesses started passing out free drinks) opened up in that way that strangers on plane rides sometimes do. "I wish I spent more time with my kids when they were little," he said. I didn't have kids yet and it almost sounded like a cliché to me at the time, but now I think I know what he means. You only get one chance at your child's infancy. You don't want to be the drunk father on the plane in twenty years lamenting what was missed… So put down this book and go bond with your baby.

THE AUTHORS

James di Properzio is a freelance writer and editor, specializing in making technical information interesting and accessible. He used to say he "probably wanted to have a kid... someday." When his wife became pregnant, James worked from home, which gave him the chance to  become a more involved dad, despite the fact that he had never held an infant before. Now James and his wife, Jennifer Margulis, have three children... so far.

Jennifer Margulis has eaten fried crickets in Niger, performed the cancan in America, and appeared on prime-time television in France. Her work has been published in *The New York Times*, *The Washington Post*, *Military History Quarterly*, *Wondertime Magazine*, and dozens  of other national and local magazines and newspapers. An award-winning writer and former Fulbright Scholar, she lives in Ashland, Oregon, with her husband and three children.

THE PHOTOGRAPHER

Christopher Briscoe photographs people from all walks of life, all over the world. His celebrity faces include Michael Douglas, Kathryn Zeta Jones, Kirk Douglas, Rob Lowe, Ray Charles, Bo Derek, and Mikhail Gorbachev. Based in the Pacific Northwest, he has published his photo-  graphs in *Time* magazine, *USA Today*, and *The Los Angeles Times*. Chris' portfolio at www.chrisbriscoe.com is an example of his connection with people and the magic light he splashes upon them. Aside from the pleasure of photographing wonderful faces, Briscoe's greatest joy comes from being a dad to his son, Quincy.